WORKBOOK
Second Edition

Jack Rabin
Professor of Public Administration and Public Policy
School of Public Affairs
The Pennsylvania State University–Harrisburg
Middletown, Pennsylvania

W. Bartley Hildreth
Regents Distinguished Professor of Public Finance
Hugo Wall School of Urban & Public Affairs
Wichita State University
Wichita, Kansas

Gerald J. Miller
Associate Professor of Public Administration
Graduate Department of Public Administration
Rutgers–The State University of New Jersey
Newark, New Jersey

CARL VINSON INSTITUTE OF GOVERNMENT
THE UNIVERSITY OF GEORGIA

Public Budgeting Laboratory Workbook, Second Edition

Editing: Inge Whittle

Design: Reid McCallister

Digital composition: Lisa Carson

Proofreading: Norma Pettigrew, Charlotte Eberhard

Publications editor: Emily Honigberg

ISBN 0-89854-180-8 — ISBN 0-89854-183-2

Foreword

The single most important policy document of any governmental jurisdiction is the annual operating budget. Traditionally, workshops and classrooms provided little opportunity for future "budgeteers" to experience budgeting successes and failures. The *Public Budgeting Laboratory* is designed to provide the knowledge and practical experience necessary for competency in budget preparation.

The *Public Budgeting Laboratory* allows participants to experience budgeting in a simulated environment. Participants learn how to analyze data relevant to budget decisions, including revenue forecasting, expenditure estimation, and budget balancing. The *Laboratory* requires both individual and collective work and fosters behavioral insights—crucial to those having to work with others on important tasks.

The *Laboratory* received extensive testing in graduate, undergraduate, and workshop applications. As a self-contained learning package, it provides step-by-step guides on developing a budget, a data supplement with five years of extensive revenue and expenditure records, and an anthology on budget formulation and execution. In addition, an instructor's manual provides suggestions on how to conduct the laboratory.

The *Public Budgeting Laboratory* results from a collaborative effort begun by the authors while they were associated with the Vinson Institute, and the first university application of the *Laboratory* occurred at the University of Georgia. Jack Rabin is professor of public administration and public policy, School of Public Affairs, The Pennsylvania State University–Harrisburg; W. Bartley Hildreth is Regents Distinguished Professor of Public Finance, Hugo Wall School of Urban & Public Affairs, Wichita State University; and Gerald J. Miller is associate professor of public administration, Graduate Department of Public Administration, Rutgers–The State University of New Jersey, at Newark.

Sam Mitchell
Interim Director
Carl Vinson Institute of Government

Contents

WORKBOOK

Second Edition

Introduction to the *Public Budgeting Laboratory*

OBJECTIVE

To gain an overview of the budgeting laboratory. To obtain an experience as close to real life as possible, participants will use an extensive collection of material on a city in developing histories, projections, and other decisions. The *Data Sourcebook,* another component of the *Public Budgeting Laboratory,* will be used for such reference unless otherwise specified.

Participants will assume the different roles of budget staff members to simulate the production of a city budget for the next fiscal year. The instructor will become the assistant to the mayor of the City and provide staff members with necessary directions for accomplishing this task.

ACTION SEQUENCE

1. Take notes on the orientation given by the instructor.
2. Read the introductory memoranda and review the budget calendar.
3. Record necessary meeting dates and deadlines on the calendar.

MAYOR'S MEMORANDUM

To: Budget Staff Members

From: Mayor

This administration was voted into office to manage City government more professionally and to install a budgeting process in the policy administration process for the first time. As you know, I considered my first step in this direction to be the release of all department heads of the prior administration.

I will name new department heads in the near future. They will add new life and vitality to what was referred to as an "Old Boys' Club."

Since this is the first year for this process, we must formulate a budget without the information sources usually necessary to allocate funds accurately. We will persevere. I have instructed the assistant to the mayor to guide you as much as possible, particularly about the new budget process we will use. I have approved the steps in this process, and my assistant will give them to you.

Let me be very clear about what I expect. First, you have very little time to complete the budget; therefore, I do not expect in-depth analyses on all issues.

Second, I want to see some relationship in budget requests between what departments do and what they spend. I realize discerning such relationships in past spending may be quite difficult, but you must make some effort to do so now.

Third, the size of the budget should depend on what is best for this community and the delivery of quality services. You must take into account the rate of inflation, the real needs of departments, and, of course, expected revenue. The budget must be balanced. Concentrate on paring any department needs that seem unwarranted.

I trust the first year of the new budget process will provide you with greater insights about city management and with a work program for further policy and issue analyses.

LETTER FROM THE ASSISTANT TO THE MAYOR

To: Budget Staff Members

From: Assistant to the Mayor

You should have reviewed already the memorandum from the mayor.

The new budgeting process has 14 steps:

Step 1: As staff members, you will review the impact of budgets on people and on organizations, terms and concepts of budgeting, major revenue sources, methods, and funds.

Step 2: You will consider the social, political, and economic characteristics of the City. In addition, you will analyze the City's revenue sources. You will review special conditions placed on the use of revenues and city-county cooperative arrangements. Moreover, you will discuss departments of the City.

Step 3: You will be assigned to analyze the expenditure experience of an individual department (or departments) of the City government. Expenditures for the last five years are to be categorized and listed by department.

Step 4: You will, as a staff, exchange completed written expenditure experience reports for all departments and make oral presentations on the expenditure histories of those departments assigned to you.

Step 5: You will review the revenue history of the City for the last five years.

Step 6: Collectively, you as staff will exchange completed revenue history reports for the City and make oral presentations on the behavior of individual revenue items over the past five years.

Step 7: The staff will discuss revenue projections for the next budget year. Each staff member must project revenues for the City as a whole. Several projection methods will be discussed.

Step 8: The staff will use a four-phased approach to present the revenue projections for the City:

> Phase 1: Written presentation of revenue projections
>
> Phase 2: Analysis of projected revenues and consultation
>
> Phase 3: Oral presentation of revenue projections
>
> Phase 4: Staff decision on revenue projections

Step 9: Those staff members whose departments have capital improvement projects for the next budget year also will prepare a capital improvements budget.

Step 10: Each of you will prepare expenditure requests for his/her department(s) for the next fiscal year. These expenditures will consist of all projected costs.

Step 11: The staff will use a four-phased approach to present the expenditure expectations of the City:

> Phase 1: Presentation of written expenditure proposals without comments
>
> Phase 2: Analysis of proposed budgets and consultation
>
> Phase 3: Oral presentation of proposed budgets
>
> Phase 4: Research and consultation

Step 12: The staff will develop a budget draft to be submitted to the assistant to the mayor. Any further differences are to be resolved, and any further expenditure justifications are to be presented at this time.

Step 13: I will critique the draft budget; and you, as budget staff, will act on my comments.

Step 14: In a feedback session, you will consider the events that occurred during the budget process as well as aspects of budgeting and decision making highlighted by your actions.

BUDGET CALENDAR		
Class	**Date**	**Step**
		Step 1: Introduction to Budgeting
		Step 2: Introduction to the City
		Step 3: Developing the Expenditure History of the City
		Step 4: Report to Staff on Expenditure Histories
		Step 5: Developing the City's Revenue History
		Step 6: Report to Staff on Revenue Histories
		Step 7: Developing Revenue Projections
		Step 8: Presentation and Analysis of Revenue Projections
		Step 9: Estimating Capital Improvements
		Step 10: Developing Expenditure Estimates
		Step 11: Presentation and Analysis of Expenditure Proposals
		Step 12: Preparation of Budget Draft
		Step 13: Comments by Assistant to the Mayor and Staff Response
		Step 14: Feedback Session—Assessing Budget Formulation and Execution

Introduction to Budgeting

OBJECTIVE

To become familiar with basic terms of financial management.

ACTION SEQUENCE

1. Read the sections on "Terms and Concepts" and "Revenue Sources" that follow.

2. In *Budgeting: Formulation and Execution,* read the following:
   a. "Introduction" to budget formulation (Part 1)
   b. Peterson, "The Three Policy Arenas"
   c. Miller, "Productivity and the Budget Process"
   d. Levine, "Cutback Management in an Era of Scarcity"
   e. Allen, "Evaluating Alternative Revenue Sources"
   f. International Association of Assessing Officers, "Property Tax and Assessment"
   g. "Introduction" to budget execution (Part 2)
   h. Forrester and Mullins, "Rebudgeting: The Serial Nature of Municipal Budgetary Processes"
   i. Grizzle, "Fund Accounting: An Introduction for Public and Nonprofit Organization Managers"

TERMS AND CONCEPTS

An understanding of certain terms is as important in the preparation of budgets as the numbers involved. Definitions for important terms follow:

Fiscal year: A 12-month period to which the annual operating budget applies and at the end of which a jurisdiction determines its financial position and the results of its operation. (The fiscal year runs from January 1 through December 31 in the City reviewed in this exercise. Thus, the calendar year [CY] serves as its fiscal year [FY].)

Operating budget: A financial plan including (1) all estimates of proposed operating and recurring expenditures for a fiscal year and (2) the proposed means for financing the expenditures.

Capital budgeting: A separate budget method, apart from the operating budget process, for use in the identifying, scheduling, and financing of buildings, land, and other large, high-cost items of a government jurisdiction. Terms frequently used in capital budgeting are defined on page 64.

Revenues: Money received by a government, not including funds received through borrowing. The essential formula for each revenue item is as follows: legal rate $\times$ [times] economic base = [equals] amount due to the government.

Expenditures: Disbursement of money to cover the expenses of a government's operations or investments in capital projects.

Fund: An account established for a specific purpose. Revenues and expenditures associated with this account are segregated and may be used only for the purposes for which the account was established.

General fund: A set of accounts for all revenues and expenditures that are not allocated to a restricted fund.

Special fund: A set of accounts for specific taxes or other earmarked revenue sources which by law are designated to finance particular functions or activities.

Fund balance: Represents what funds are left after claims against a city are subtracted from the things of value held by a city. The essential formula is as follows: revenues and other sources of funds $-$ [less] expenditures and other uses of funds = [equals] the fund balance.

Accounting system: The records and procedures used to record, classify, and report financial information.

Budget document: The instrument used to present the comprehensive financial plan of a government jurisdiction.

Appropriation: A designated amount of public money that a government's legislative body has authorized to be spent for specific purposes during a prescribed period of time. It is illegal to spend money that has not been appropriated.

REVENUE SOURCES

Many different sources of revenue are available for use by governments. Based on common characteristics, each revenue source can be placed into a category. Possible categories are:

    A. Taxes
    B. Licenses and Permits
    C. Charges for Services
    D. Fines and Forfeits
    E. Intergovernmental Revenue
    F. Other Revenue

Individual revenue sources that might be placed within the categories are as follows:

A. Taxes

General real property (ad valorem) tax
Personal property (ad valorem) tax
Motor vehicle (ad valorem) tax
Sales and use tax
Gross receipts business tax
Beer and wine excise tax
Liquor tax
Gasoline tax
Tobacco tax
Occupational license tax
Amusement tax
Lodging tax
Utilities earnings tax

B. Licenses and Permits

Business licenses, permits, and fees
Inspection fees
Building, electrical, and plumbing permits
Franchise fees

C. Charges for Services

Court costs, fees, and charges
Equipment rental and installation charges
Ambulance fees
Zoning and subdivision fees
Parking meter and garage receipts
Water charges
Garbage collection charges
Sewer charges
Recreation facility charges
Library charges
Sprinkler system and fire hydrant rent

D. Fines and Forfeits

Court fines and forfeits

E. Intergovernmental Revenue

1. State-shared revenue
   Banking institutions' gross receipts and excise tax
   State gasoline tax
   Motor vehicle licenses

2. State grants
   Recreation
   Law enforcement

3. Federal grants

4. County-shared revenue
County beer tax

5. County payments for city-administered services
Fire protection

F. Other Revenue

Interest earnings
Interest on late tax payments
Rents
Cemetery lot sales
Contributions from utility enterprises operated by an independent board
Sale of excess property
Royalties

Introduction to the City

OBJECTIVE

To become acquainted with the City by researching general factors such as socioeconomic growth and specific factors such as revenue sources. The *Data Sourcebook* provides information on these factors.

ACTION SEQUENCE

1. Familiarize yourself with the City by reading the introductory characteristics presented in the *Data Sourcebook.*

2. After reading information on the City's form of government and intergovernmental relations in the *Data Sourcebook,* answer questions about the City on *Workbook* page 12.

3. Read information on the socioeconomic characteristics of the City and on the relationship between the City and the county in the *Data Sourcebook* and do the *Workbook* exercise on page 13.

4. In *Budgeting: Formulation and Execution,* read the following:
   a. Morgan, "Local Government Structure"
   b. Advisory Commission on Intergovernmental Relations, "States and Their Local Governments"
   c. Department of the Treasury, "Principles of Fiscal Federalism"
   d. Oakerson, "Local Public Economies: Provision, Production and Governance"
   e. Galambos and Schreiber, "Economic Base: What Our Jobs Are Tied To"
   f. Advisory Commission on Intergovernmental Relations, "Mandates: Cases in State-Local Relations"
   g. The District of Columbia Tax Revision Commission, "Criteria for Evaluating a (Revenue) System"

5. Consider the roles ascribed to the municipality and answer questions in the *Workbook* on page 14.

6. Answer questions dealing with the local government's tax and economic bases in the *Workbook,* page 15.

7. Refer to specific revenue sources of the City, identified in the *Data Sourcebook,* and answer questions on *Workbook* page 16.

8. Review the specific limits on indebtedness applicable to the City presented in the *Data Sourcebook.* Answer questions on revenues and revenue use and on limits to indebtedness, *Workbook* page 18.

9. Examine *Data Sourcebook* for the names of City departments.

FORM OF GOVERNMENT

Budgeting occurs within the political and organizational structure of a city. That is, a budget is the result of interpersonal conflict and bargaining; moreover, the budget's structure is a "mirror" of the organizational structure of a city. Thus, it is important to understand the City's form of government.

What form of government does the City have?

What is the role of the city council?

Who else has some responsibility in developing the budget?

SOCIOECONOMIC CHARACTERISTICS

Information on the socioeconomic characteristics of the City provides a perspective on the conditions under which public budgeting operates.

Describe the City's socioeconomic characteristics:

1. population

2. economic base:

    a. Using the article by Galambos and Schreiber on economic base, analyze Table 13 in the *Data Sourcebook* to determine export employment

        (1) Is the economic base diverse?

        (2) Is export employment growing?

    b. Using the *Data Sourcebook,* analyze the university's contribution to the economic base.

3. land use

4. natural resources

Summarize data in concise statements. Relate the effect of change in each characteristic to the development of the City's budget for the past five years. Considering past trends, what will affect the City's budget during the next five years?

Characteristic	Information	Past Effect of Change	Future Effect

(Use more sheets as needed.)

13

ROLE OF LOCAL GOVERNMENT

The limits of governmental action and the importance of private markets raise questions about the role of local governments in the local economy.

What goods and services can a local government provide to enhance the economic interests of its population?

How can public goods and services be produced without direct public delivery?

TAX BASE

Describe the tax base on which the City depends for raising local revenues. Be sure to note whether the economic base (the source of jobs, income for citizens, and tax revenue for the City) is expanding or contracting.

(Use more sheets as needed.)

SOURCES OF REVENUE

A necessary feature of public budgeting concerns the range of revenue-generating devices permissible under law. Comparison between all legally permissible revenue sources and ones currently selected for use provides a consideration for future budget decisions. In addition, it is important to understand the linkage of each revenue structure to its economic base.

What revenue sources are currently used in the City and what is the economic activity underlying that revenue source?

(Use more sheets as needed.)

List any legally permissible revenue sources the City does not utilize currently.

(Use more sheets as needed.)

CHANGES IN CURRENT REVENUE SOURCES: SPECIAL CONDITIONS PLACED ON USE OF REVENUES AND INDEBTEDNESS

For each revenue item used in the City, find out the following information (consult *Budgeting: Formulation and Execution* readings on "Budget Setting") cited in the **Action Sequence** for this step, items 4 (f) and (g). Also use *Data Sourcebook* descriptions of earmarked revenues and conditions of indebtedness:

A. Concerning scope and limitations on use, e.g., which revenues are earmarked for specific uses and which are not, what percentage of total revenues collected consists of earmarked revenues?

B. What are the impacts of a change in a tax rate or fee level, and have there been any recent changes?

C. Are there any revenue items whose rates the city has the legal authority to raise?

D. What special conditions are placed on the different types of indebtedness?

(Use more sheets as needed.)

Developing the Expenditure History of the City

OBJECTIVE

To grasp the nature of City operations by researching the expenditure histories of City departments for the past five years. You look at past budget behavior to give some indication for judging the current budget year. You become a staff specialist for one or more departments, examining each in detail.

ACTION SEQUENCE

1. Receive assignments from instructor on department study responsibility and list them on *Workbook* page 20.

2. Review "Expenditure Categories" and "Nondepartmental Costs," pages 21-22.

3. Examine assigned departmental data in the *Data Sourcebook,* using methods presented on *Workbook* page 23.

4. Develop a five-year profile of line-item expenditures for departments assigned, on Form 1, using information from the *Data Sourcebook* (See *Workbook* pp. 24-26.)

5. Analyze the spending history of the assigned departments by answering questions on pages 27 and 28.

6. In *Budgeting: Formulation and Execution,* read the following:
   a. Sanders and Tyer, "Local Government Financial and Budgetary Analysis"
   b. Carney and Schoenfeld, "How to Read a Budget"

7. Read Ammons, "Adjusting for Inflation When Comparing Revenues or Expenditures," and convert expenditures to constant dollars using procedure in *Workbook* (p. 29) and Table 15 in the *Data Sourcebook.*

8. Prepare a variance analysis for each assigned department as described on page 30.

9. Read Groves, Godsey, and Shulman, "Financial Indicators for Local Government," and develop relevant expenditure ratios in the exercise on page 31.

ASSIGNMENT OF DEPARTMENTS

Each member of the budget staff is assigned one or more City departments and asked to determine the previous expenditures for each department.

The expenditure history of the City includes all expenditures for all programs for the past five years. All expenditures for special programs with funding coming from state or federal sources or through a special fund must be included.

Department Assignments:

1. _____

2. _____

3. _____

4. _____

5. _____

6. _____

EXPENDITURE HISTORIES

To develop department expenditure histories, budget line items from year to year can be grouped using a number of different formats. The *Data Sourcebook* provides data to be used in developing this expenditure experience.

Expenditure Categories

With this format, all costs necessary for operating a particular function or department of the municipality can be placed into one of the following categories:

A. Salaries
B. Supplies
C. Services
D. Equipment
E. Capital Improvements/Capital Outlays
F. Nondepartmental Costs

The line items used by each department of the City for the past five years fit within the following categories as shown:

A. Salaries

Salaries and wages
Overtime

Note: Fringe benefits are covered under section "F"

B. Supplies

Recreation supplies
Office supplies
Clothing
Food
Gas, oil, and lubricants
Building and construction materials
Vehicle repair materials and supplies
Ammunition
Street repair material/supplies
Chemicals
Janitorial supplies

C. Services

Commercial contractor's service
Telephone and telegraph costs
Postage
Advertising
Printing
Electric power and other utility costs
Travel, conferences, and meetings
Repairs to vehicles, equipment, and buildings

Rent

User fees charged by another government for use of its landfill, etc.

D. Equipment—expenditures of relatively low cost, rapidly depreciating items of equipment paid in one fiscal year, such as—

Typewriters
Accounting machines
Tools
Vehicles

E. Capital Improvements/Capital Outlays—expenditures for new or expanded physical facilities that are large-scale, expensive, and/or relatively permanent, such as—

Street improvements
Sewer and water system expansions
Buildings
Land
Recreation site improvements
Fire apparatuses

(Items in category "E" are capital improvement projects; therefore, they will be included in the capital budget discussed in more detail in Step 9.)

F. Nondepartmental Costs—expense items only indirectly related to a particular department or function and not easily charged against any one function. They are usually distinguishable by their fixed nature from one year to the next. In the City, these costs are charged to a consolidated account called General/Administrative. Examples of nondepartmental costs in the City are—

Social security ("FICA" taxes)
Pensions and retirement contributions
Workers' compensation
Other employee benefits
Insurance (life, health, casualty)
Contributions to other agencies (school board, county health department, county library)
Dues to organizations (statewide municipal association, regional commission)
Retirement of debt
Interest on debt
Trustee fees for financial advisors who administer bond issues
Judgments
Internal service funds (for goods or services provided by one department to another, e.g., service garage)

Note: Certain professional services normally charged to a nondepartmental section will be contained in a department's expenditure list (auditing, legal, engineering, and consultants).

EXPENDITURE ANALYSIS

There are a variety of ways to gain an understanding of a series of data. In this step, you will examine expenditures by using each of these methods:

1. Dollar changes, over the (five-year) time series.
2. Percentage change, over the time series.
3. Proportion, or share, of the budget, over the time series.
4. Constant dollar changes, over the time series.
5. Comparison of each year's budget to actual results, and over the time series.
6. Ratios of expenditures to social and economic factors, over the time series.

Be sure to use visual aids (pie charts, graphs, etc.) to help illustrate trends.

DEPARTMENTAL EXPENDITURES

What were your department's expenditures for previous years?

To develop a five-year profile of line-item expenditures, list each line item by category and subtotal. A table format similar to the one found in Form 1 should be constructed. The sample Form 1 includes mock data for several categories; a blank Form 1 is included for student use.

(*Note*: More data exist than can be placed on the forms included in this *Workbook*. Be sure to photocopy additional copies of each blank form before using.)

Recommended categories:

Salaries

Supplies

Services

Equipment

Capital Outlays/Capital Improvements

Nondepartmental Costs (if any)

After organizing all line items by category, add all line-item amounts to get a subtotal for each category.

Data for completing Form 1 is found in the *Data Sourcebook* in the department/account title section. Do not show cents; round off to dollars.

In addition, calculate the relative change from one year to another using the following percentage change formula:

$$\frac{\text{Later Year} - \text{Earlier Year}}{\text{Earlier Year}} \times 100$$

Round off percentages to two decimals.

Two rules help in this regard:

1. If the dollars in the later year are *more* than the dollars in the earlier year, it is a *percent* increase.

2. If the dollars in the later year are *less* than the dollars in the earlier year, it is a *percent* decrease.

FORM 1 (example)

Expenditures and Percentage Changes
Department: Public Works

Categories and Line Items	FY I $	FY II $	Percent Change	FY III $	Percent Change	FY IV $	Percent Change	FY V $	Percent Change
Salaries									
Salaries	40,103	39,537	1.4	56,816	44	67,637	19	75,603	12
Subtotal	40,103	39,537	1.4	56,816	44	67,637	19	75,603	12
Supplies									
Office supplies	200	532	165	947	78	1,074	13	883	18
Tools and supplies	7	0	(100)	0	NA	0	NA	0	NA
Subtotal	207	532	156	947	78	1,074	13	883	(18)
Services									
Telephone	87	0	(100)	1,015	100	1,338	32	1,639	23
Freight and express	0	0	NA	0	NA	3	100	0	(100)
Printing	0	0	NA	0	NA	97	100	358	266
Advertising	0	0	NA	0	NA	52	100	0	(100)
Equip. repair	0	0	NA	0	NA	54	100	212	289
Prof. services	9,038	7,200	(20)	7,200	0	7,200	0	5,400	(25)
Car allowance	0	0	NA	1,700	100	0	(100)	0	NA
Travel	0	0	NA	0	NA	2,551	100	2,435	(4.5)
Dues and subscripts	0	0	NA	0	NA	76	100	0	(100)
Training	0	0	NA	0	NA	0	NA	533	100
Subtotal	9,125	7,200	(21)	9,915	38	11,371	15	10,577	(7)
Capital	0	0	NA	0	NA	972	100	0	(100)
Subtotal	0	0	NA	0	NA	972	100	0	(100)
Total	49,435	47,269	(4)	67,678	43	81,054	20	87,063	7

FORM 1

Your Name _____

Expenditures and Percentage Changes
Department: _____

Categories and Line Items	FY I $	FY II $	Percent Change	FY III $	Percent Change	FY IV $	Percent Change	FY V $	Percent Change

ANALYZING THE EXPENDITURE EXPERIENCE

Analyze each of your departments using the following questions and include the answers to these questions as an addendum to Form 1:

1. What are each department's major spending categories and line items for the five-year period?

2. What are the major variances from year to year?

(Use more sheets as needed.)

SHARES OF THE BUDGET

The allocation of funds may reveal preferences by those who develop budgets. One way to learn about priorities is to look at the proportion that one item is of the total. To some, this is also termed "common size form."

The formula for determining how much one item is in proportion to the whole is

$$\frac{\text{Dollars for One Item in a Series}}{\text{Dollars for All Items in a Series}} \times 100.$$

Example:

	FY V	
	Dollars	**Proportion (%)**
Salaries	$75,603	86.84
Supplies	883	1.01
Services	10,577	12.15
Capital Improvements	0	0
	$87,063	100%

If used for all years of data (by line item), this technique reveals changes in priorities over time. Columns showing what proportion of the total expenditures each line item (excluding the subtotals) represents can be added to Form 1.

1. What changes occurred in the budget shares within each department?

2. What might account for the specific changes you noted (new positions, one-time expenditures, etc.)?

EXPENDITURES CONVERTED TO CONSTANT DOLLARS

The same dollar amount in different years can have a different purchasing value. This results because of price changes. Current, or nominal dollars, can be converted to reflect underlying price changes. Price indexes, which measure changes in the prices of a "market basket" of goods and services purchased by similar buyers, are generally available.[1]

Evaluate the expenditure history in terms of constant dollars, i.e., controlling for price changes. Use the following formula:

$$\text{Constant Dollar Expenditures} = \frac{\text{Expenditures}}{\text{Consumer Price Index}} \times 100$$
$$\textbf{or } \text{Implicit Price Deflator}$$

Expenditure Example:

	Current Dollars	Implicit Price Deflator	Constant Dollars
Year I	$5,000	100*	$5,000
Year II	6,500	110	5,909**

---

*Assuming YEAR I serves as the year when the IPD = 100.

**Meaning that Year II current expenditures of $6,500 translate into only $5,909 in Year I dollar terms.

Make this calculation for total departmental expenditures.

1. What changes are revealed once price effects are removed from expenditure data?

---

[1]See *Survey of Current Business,* published monthly by the U.S. Department of Commerce. The *Data Sourcebook* contains the price index for the laboratory City in the "Overview of the City."

COMPARING THE BUDGET TO ACTUAL RESULTS

A public budget is a legal plan for what will likely happen over the 12 months of expenditures. Comparing the budgeted amount to actual year-end results reveals the ability of officials to implement the budget plan. Despite the best intentions, plans change, revenues do not materialize, and other events intervene to require rebudgeting.

A table such as the one below examines *within-the-year* budget variance. Specifically, it permits the analyst to assess how well the forecasted start-of-year "budget" amount relates to the end-of-year "actual" amount. A zero variance would indicate perfect budget implementation (in aggregate dollar terms), while more than 100 percent would indicate over-budget (more spent than budgeted) and less than 100 percent would indicate under-budget (less spent than budgeted).

Budget to Actual—Variance Analysis
Department XYZ

Category	Budgeted Amount	Actual Amount	Variance in Percentage
Salaries	$100	$110	110
Supplies	100	90	90
Services	100	100	100
Capital	0	0	
Total	$300	$300	100

Prepare a variance analysis for each of your departments and comment on what the results show.

EXPENDITURE RATIO ANALYSIS

It helps to view one amount in association with another, thus the concept of ratios. The most frequent ratios are per capita amounts.

First, divide total departmental expenditures in each year by the city's population that year to derive the ratio of expenditures per capita. Then, do the same calculation but use *constant* dollar expenditures.

What observations emerge from the use of these ratios?

Report to Staff on Expenditure Histories

OBJECTIVE

To present other staff members with a spending history of your assigned departments.

ACTION SEQUENCE

1. Compile the expenditure history of your assigned departments in a written report. Make extra copies and give them to others to study. Include a completed Form 1 in your report.

2. Prepare and present an oral report on the analysis of expenditures, recording the outline of your oral report (see p. 33). Take notes on others' oral reports using page 34 and adding extra pages as needed. Staff should next compare expenditure histories of all the departments (see p. 35).

EXPENDITURE HISTORY

Rehearsing your presentation of material will help you to collect your thoughts, pinpoint important elements, and organize data. Use this space to plan your presentation.

Your presentation should concentrate on the information that you developed when you analyzed the expenditure experiences of each department.

1. What are the department's major spending categories and line items for the five-year period?
2. What are the major variations from year to year?
3. How were line-item listings (definitions) changed over time and what does this do for budget planning?
4. How will past spending trends likely influence next year's budget plans?

Be sure to have the above information for each department.

(Use more sheets as needed.)

Record here your thoughts on others' presentations of spending histories. Give special attention to data dealing with departments that might have some bearing upon your areas.

(Use more sheets as needed.)

COMPARISON OF DEPARTMENTAL EXPENDITURE HISTORIES

The staff should compare departmental expenditure histories and deal with questions such as which departments have had the greatest salary and/or capital improvement changes over the last five years; which departments' total expenditures have been growing; and, how much of the total City expenditures is each department's? How have the various departments held up in constant dollar terms? Compare budget-to-actual results across departments.

(Use more sheets as needed.)

STEP 5 — Developing the City's Revenue History

OBJECTIVE

To understand the nature of City revenues by researching the history of each source of City funds for the past five years. As a budget staff member, research the revenue history of *all* funds.

ACTION SEQUENCE

1. Receive assignments from instructor on revenue source study responsibilities.

2. Review the information on revenue sources in the *Data Sourcebook*.

3. Develop a five-year history of collections by revenue source, using information from the *Data Sourcebook*. Compile this information on *Workbook* pages 37 and 39.

4. Analyze City revenue history by listing revenue sources and answering questions on pages 40 and 41.

5. In *Budgeting: Formulation and Execution,* read the following selections *or* review those previously assigned.

    a. The District of Columbia Tax Revision Commission, "Criteria for Evaluating a (Revenue) System"

    b. International Association of Assessing Officers, "Property Tax and Assessment"

    c. Ammons, "Adjusting for Inflation When Comparing Revenues or Expenditures"

    d. Allan, "Evaluating Alternative Revenue Sources"

    e. Neels and Caggiano, "Pricing Public Services"

REVENUE HISTORY

Develop a five-year history report of each of the City's line-item revenue sources. You should group these line-item sources of revenue by their common characteristics. Use the categories listed on pages 7-9 to group line items, and use a tabular format similar to the one found in Form 2. A completed sample form is shown on page 38. Attach a copy of the report to this volume.

As with expenditures, there are a variety of ways to study revenue data, so use the same methods here:

1. Dollar changes, over the time series (in nominal terms).

2. Percentage change, over the time series.

3. Proportion, or share, of all revenues, over the time series.

4. Constant dollar change, over the time series.

5. Comparison of each year's budget to actual results, and over the time series.

6. Ratios of revenues to social and economic factors, over the time series.

Use the general descriptions of each of the above methods contained in Step 3, the development of an expenditure history step. Be sure to record the results of your analyses. Visual aids (e.g., pie charts, graphs) can also help illustrate trends.

FORM 2 (example)

Revenues and Percentage Change

Categories and Line Items	FY I $	FY II $	Percent Change	FY III $	Percent Change	FY IV $	Percent Change	FY V $	Percent Change
Taxes									
Ad valorem (property)	1,065,569	1,147,034	7.65	1,665,384	45.19	2,342,225	40.64	1,545,827	(34.00)
Ad valorem (motor veh.)	81,885	91,430	11.66	93,383	2.14	84,484	(9.53)	93,255	10.38
Spec. taxes and licenses	683,178	689,341	.90	710,544	3.08	754,266	6.15	841,870	11.61
Gross earnings—Power Co.	261,102	298,481	14.32	358,923	20.25	487,749	35.89	490,007	.46
Gross earnings—Gas Co.	64,647	62,065	(3.99)	78,505	26.49	85,229	8.56	110,735	29.93
Beer and wine excise	376,867	446,432	18.46	581,684	11.49	648,519	11.49	684,399	5.53
Whiskey excise	98,751	95,075	(3.72)	94,131	(.99)	97,794	3.89	103,354	5.69
Intangible	14,122	10,411	(26.28)	26,444	153.9	22,983	(13.09)	27,580	20.00
Hotel and motel	0	0		17,503		57,758	229.98	69,621	20.54
Subtotal	2,646,121	2,840,269	7.34	3,626,501	27.68	4,581,007	26.32	3,966,648	(13.41)
Licenses and Permits									
Cable TV	11,817	10,300	(12.84)	13,340	29.51	15,288	14.61	16,159	5.70
Planning comm. permits	107	0		0		0		0	
Subtotal	11,924	10,300	(13.63)	13,340	29.51	15,288	14.61	16,159	5.70
Charges for Services									
Water revenue	2,150,214	2,239,451	4.15	2,213,000	(1.18)	2,509,845	13.41	2,741,925	9.25
Water meters	50,557	45,467	9.87	29,899	(34.39)	42,401	41.81	51,376	21.17
Sewage rent	588,245	611,014	3.87	812,471	32.97	929,458	14.40	970,437	4.41
Stub outs—water and sewer	75,490	60,148	(20.32)	31,365	(47.85)	77,834	148.16	60,437	(22.35)
Subtotal	2,864,506	2,956,080	3.20	3,086,735	4.42	3,559,538	15.32	3,824,175	7.43

FORM 2

Your Name _____

Revenues and Percentage Change

Categories and Line Items	Year I $	Year II $	Percent Change	Year III $	Percent Change	Year IV $	Percent Change	Year V $	Percent Change

ANALYZING CITY REVENUE HISTORY

What revenue sources have varied the most and what factors might account for the changes (e.g., rate change, economic base change, etc.)?

Include this listing and the answers to the questions on page 41 as an addendum to Form 2.

Significant Revenue Sources That Have Changed	Reasons for Change?

FEATURES OF REVENUE STRUCTURE AND BEHAVIOR

There are numerous aspects of city revenues with which you need to be familiar. Answer the following questions using information from "Socioeconomic Characteristics" and "City Fiscal Characteristics" of the *Data Sourcebook*.

1. Recurring revenues are items available from one year to the next, barring any change in law or policy. Budget experts generally discourage the use of nonrecurring revenues for use in funding recurring expenditures, since such funds may not materialize at all or be available in succeeding fiscal periods. What revenues are recurring and what revenues are nonrecurring?

2. Unearmarked revenues are items not assigned for use for a particular purpose. Revenues are earmarked by law, contract, or policy. An earmarked revenue cannot be used to fund any expenditure for which it is not authorized. Which revenues are earmarked and which are not?

3. An elastic revenue source is one responsive to a change in its base. Usually stated as revenue elasticity, this means that for every 1 percent increase (decrease) in the local economy's personal income, receipts from that tax rise (fall) by more than 1 percent. Revenue source elasticity is calculated by revenue change (Year 2 minus Year 1, for example) divided by personal income change (Year 2 minus Year 1). (Highly elastic revenue sources help avoid the need for frequent tax rate and/or tax base changes. The problem is that such taxes are subject to declines [increases] during economic recession [or growth or inflationary] periods.) Which revenue sources are elastic in nature?

Report to Staff on Revenue Histories

OBJECTIVE

To present other staff members with a revenue history of the City.

ACTION SEQUENCE

1. Compile the revenue history of the City in a written report, making extra copies for others to study. Include a completed Form 2 (from Step 5) in your report.

2. Prepare an oral report on the analysis of revenue collections, record the outline of the oral report, and report to others on your analysis. Use page 43, adding extra pages as needed, to plan your presentation.

3. Take notes on others' oral reports and discuss the differences. Resolve possible differences in revenue histories so as to have one consensus revenue history for the City. (See pp. 44 and 45.)

4. Appoint a staff member to record the consensus revenue history of the City as each revenue line item is discussed.

PRESENTATION OF REVENUE HISTORY

Use this space to plan your presentation.

    You should be familiar, by revenue line item, with the following:

        a. Is the revenue source recurring or nonrecurring, earmarked or nonearmarked?

        b. How has the revenue item varied from year to year? Has there been extreme variation, either up or down?

        c. What City socioeconomic characteristic(s) might be responsible for the variation(s) found in the revenue line item? How vulnerable are taxes to economic recession (inflation)?

        d. How will past revenue trends likely influence next year's budget plans?

(Use more sheets as needed.)

Record here your thoughts on others' presentations of revenue histories.

(Use more sheets as needed.)

Discuss any differences between your revenue presentation and those of others.

Developing Revenue Projections

OBJECTIVE

To project future City revenues, choose a projections method for each line-item revenue source from several discussed in the section. Those mentioned are most commonly used today by governments.

ACTION SEQUENCE

1. Read the revenue projection methods in this section: use of proportionate-change, moving averages, and least-squares trend-line methods.

2. Make revenue projections for each source of City revenue on Form 3 (p. 56), provide your rationale on Form 3A (p. 57), and photocopy them for later distribution.

3. Read Liner, "Projecting Local Government Revenue," in *Budgeting: Formulation and Execution.*

PROJECTING REVENUE

To estimate revenue collections for an upcoming fiscal year, you must follow certain procedures. These include

1. projecting each line-item revenue source separately;

2. accounting for seasonal fluctuations and out-of-the-ordinary changes in past collections of each revenue source;

3. anticipating, if possible, any problems in the collection of a specific revenue source; and

4. projecting each individual revenue source in a conservative manner.

Revenue estimating is important since you want to avoid a deficit when you complete the budget. However, try to arrive at the most accurate, yet conservative, estimate you can obtain rather than intentionally under- or overestimating.

The following questions will help you assess the revenue picture and choose the projection method to use:

1. Are increases from the revenue sources linked directly to economic growth (retail sales, housing starts, and personal income, for example) and annual increases in City population? (Examine ad valorem taxes, gross receipt taxes, sales taxes, and business license fees to gain clues.)

2. Can any large increase in a particular revenue source from one year to the next be attributed to a rate change, a new way of billing, or to an external factor, such as inflation, that may give the appearance of growth?

Use of Proportionate-Change Method

An analysis of previous years' collections can be used to develop a reasonably conservative estimate for the next year's collections. Some small communities use the proportionate-change method to accomplish this.

The proportionate-change method can be used if (1) the revenue source has been used for the past few years and (2) if there are records of its collections during those years.

Example

The sequence of procedures required in the proportionate-change method, using revenue from business licenses as examples, is as follows:

Suppose City Alpha has records indicating these previous collections of the business license fees:

Fiscal Year	Collections ($)
FY A	23,000
FY B	24,300
FY C	27,300
FY D	30,300
FY E	34,300
FY F (present year)	38,800

Step 1

Find the difference in collections between each year. For example, the difference between FY B and FY C is:

$27,300 (FY C)
$$
\begin{array}{r}
\underline{-24{,}300 \ (\text{FY B})} \\
\$\ 3{,}000 \ (\text{difference})
\end{array}
$$

Step 2

To find the percentage change, divide the difference by the first year's collections. For example:

$$\frac{\$\ 3{,}000}{24{,}300} = .1234 \text{ or } 12.34\%$$

Step 3

Repeat steps 1 and 2 for the other yearly pairs and record the answers. Total the percentage changes, rounding to the closest percent.

Year	Collections ($)	Change (%)
FY A	23,000	
FY B	24,300	12.34
FY C	27,300	
FY D	30,300	
FY E	34,300	
FY F	38,800	

Step 4

Compare your answers to the following correct listing.

Year	Collections ($)	Change (%)
FY A	23,000	5.65
FY B	24,300	12.34
FY C	27,300	10.99
FY D	30,300	13.20
FY E	34,300	13.11
FY F	38,800	
	Total Change	55.29

Step 5

The most conservative estimate for the upcoming year's revenue collections results from averaging the present change for the given six fiscal years. First, determine the number of percentage changes. This example has five changes:

FY A to FY B; FY B to FY C; FY C to FY D; FY D to FY E; FY E to FY F.

To determine the average percentage change, follow this process:
Take the total percentage change (55 percent) given in Step 4 and divide it by the number of percentage changes—5. Thus,

$$\frac{55}{5} = 11\%$$

11 percent is the average change in revenue collections for the past six fiscal years.

Step 6

With the compiled information, you can now project the collections for FY G.

First, multiply the collections for FY F ($38,800) by the average percentage change (11 percent).

$$
\begin{array}{r}
\$38,800 \\
\times \quad .11 \\
\hline
\$\ 4,268
\end{array}
$$

48

The amount ($4,268) is the expected increase for FY G over the total collection received in FY F.

Finally, the total collections from business licenses for the upcoming fiscal year (FY G) are estimated to be:

$38,800 (collected in FY F)
+ 4,268 (increase expected)
$43,068 (total collections expected for FY G)

Step 7

The projected FY G collections are based on an 11 percent increase over FY F and a net increase of $4,268. By using the proportionate-change method, a conservative growth rate has been presumed in comparison to the most immediate preceding year and more in line with the past five years. In FY F, the average percent of change was 13 percent ($4,500) over FY E.

However, an assumption was made that there were no significant changes in the tax rates, collection procedures, or economic conditions for the six fiscal years under review. Neither were any changes expected to occur during the upcoming fiscal year. If any significant changes had occurred, the projections would have been reconsidered in light of those changes.

NOTE: Two problems may occur when using the proportionate-change method. These problems involve handling (1) large fluctuations in collections over past years and (2) a drop in collections from one year to the next. Below are the problems and possible ways to handle them.

1. If revenues have fluctuated greatly over the six-year period, the average percentage increase may be too high. If revenues have had a low rate of increase for the most recent years, it may be wiser to use a rate lower than average to make a projection for the total six-year period.

2. If revenues have dropped in some years while increasing in others, it may be best to use the following procedure:
   a. Determine the average increase (or decrease) in revenue collections over the six-year period.
   b. Examine the yearly amounts to determine whether there are any extreme increases or decreases that would preclude using the six-year average.

Use of Moving Averages

A problem with the proportionate-change technique is that it treats each year of data as if the change is fundamental, meaning that minor variations can influence the next year's forecast. The moving averages method eliminates that problem by using some of the most recent, actual data to generate a forecast.

Example

Using the same example as before, City Alpha has records indicating that previous collections of the business license fees were as follows:

FY A	$23,000
FY B	$24,300
FY C	$27,300
FY D	$30,300
FY E	$34,300
FY F	$38,800

Step 1

Decide the number of periods for the average. The fewer the number, the more responsive the forecast to variations. The more years covered by the average, the more the time series will be "smoothed," and less responsive to real change. A two- or three-period average is more appropriate for a limited data set, such as in the following example.

Step 2

If a two-period average is selected, the calculations for an average for each two-period segment of the time series would reveal:

Year	Actual ($)	Calculation	Forecast for the Next Year
FY A	23,000		
FY B	24,300	$\dfrac{23,000 + 24,300}{2}$	= 23,650
FY C	27,300	$\dfrac{24,300 + 27,300}{2}$	= 25,800
FY D	30,300	$\dfrac{27,300 + 30,300}{2}$	= 28,800
FY E	34,300	$\dfrac{30,300 + 34,300}{2}$	= 32,300
FY F	38,800	$\dfrac{34,300 + 38,800}{2}$	= 36,550

Step 3

As shown, the forecasted amount for the next year (FY G) equals the moving average result from FY E and FY F. This forecasted amount ($36,550) can be compared to the amount forecasted using the previously detailed proportionate-change method ($43,068). A sensitivity analysis might be performed, running another calculation, this time using a three-period moving average. The analyst then has to decide which result is the most appropriate one to use.

Upon further examination, the proportionate-change method seems to offset FY A's small increase with the double digit increases in later years. In contrast, the moving average tends to smooth the results of two years, assuming that any single year might give a false indicator of underlying strength.

Step 4

The moving average method provides a forecast for each period (after the first two), so the difference between the forecasted amount and the actual amount can serve as another tool of the analyst. Moving averages can be used for any time series (hourly, daily, monthly, or yearly).

Use of a Least-Squares Trend Line*

You can also analyze each revenue source by using the least-squares method of developing a trend line, a more "conservative" way of projecting than the proportionate-change method. Calculation of a trend line lets the analyst better estimate future revenues, but note that the trend line should serve only as the basis for making revenue projections. Accepting the future trend-line position as the revenue projection is to assume that the trend will not change in the future.

To illustrate the sequence of procedures involved in using the least-squares trend-line method, an example that analyzes future collections from sales tax is used.

Example

Suppose City Beta had records to indicate that previous collections of sales tax were as shown:

Fiscal Year (FY)	Collections
FY A	$142,800
FY B	105,800
FY C	166,500
FY D	173,000
FY E (present year)	213,900
Total	$802,000

Step 1

Identify the central year. When there is an odd number of years, as is the case here, the middle year is the central year. (Liner's article also explains which year is central when working with an even number of years.*)

Fiscal Year (FY)	Years from Central Year
FY A	−2
FY B	−1
FY C	0
FY D	+1
FY E	+2

Step 2

Calculate the value of cross-products $[(B) \times (C)]$ and years squared $(C)^2$

*Revised from Charles D. Liner, "Projecting Local Government Revenue," *Popular Government* 43, no. 4 (Spring 1978), 32-38, 45.

Fiscal Year (A)	Collections (B)	Years from Central Year (C)	Cross-Products (B) × (C)	Years Squared (C) × (C)
FY A	$142,800	−2	−285.6	4
FY B	105,800	−1	−105.8	1
FY C	166,500	0	0	0
FY D	173,000	+1	+173.0	1
FY E	213,900	+2	+427.8	4
Total	$802,000		+209.4	10

Step 3

Calculate the slope.

$$\text{Slope} = \frac{\text{cross-products total}}{\text{years squared total}} = \frac{209.4}{10} = +20.9$$

Step 4

Calculate the level in the central year.

$$\text{Level in central year} = \frac{\text{total collections}}{\text{number of years}} = \frac{802.0}{5} = 160.40$$

Step 5

After calculating the level in the central year and the slope, you can compute the values of the trend line for each fiscal year in the past series and project the trend line to future years. Projections for FY F and FY G are shown in the following example:

Fiscal Year	Level in Central Year		Number of Years from Central Year		Slope		Trend-Line Value
FY A	160.4	+	(−2	×	20.9)	=	118.6
FY B	160.4	+	(−1	×	20.9)	=	139.5
FY C	160.4	+	(0	×	20.9)	=	160.4
FY D	160.4	+	(+1	×	20.9)	=	181.3
FY E	160.4	+	(+2	×	20.9)	=	202.2
FY F	160.4	+	(+3	×	20.9)	=	223.1
FY G	160.4	+	(+4	×	20.9)	=	244.0

Step 6

A. Graph paper helps show the relevance of the least-squares approach. Label the graph paper with the X-axis representing each fiscal year and the Y-axis representing collections.

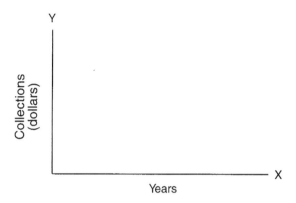

B. Plot actual revenue collections on the graph (see collections column in Step 2).

C. Plot the trend-line values for FY E and the projections for FY F and FY G (see trend-line value column in Step 5). Connect the points with a straight line.

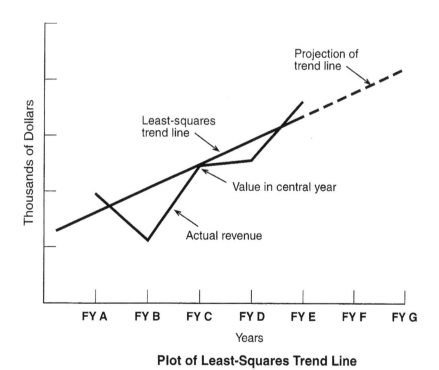

Plot of Least-Squares Trend Line

Step 7

The trend line can be used to project future revenues; however, the projection is based on the assumption that the trend will not change. A way to handle this projection problem is to adjust the data for trend using the following formula:

$$\frac{\text{actual collections}}{\text{calculated trend values}} \times 100 = \text{percentage of trend}$$

Calculation of Percentage of Trend

Fiscal Year	Actual Collections ($)		Calculated Trend Value ($)				Percentage of Trend
FY A	(142,800	–	118.6)	×	100	=	120.4
FY B	(105,800	–	139.6)	×	100	=	75.8
FY C	(166,500	–	160.4)	×	100	=	103.8
FY D	(173,000	–	181.3)	×	100	=	95.4
FY E	(213,000	–	202.2)	×	100	=	105.3

Variations of the actual data from the trend line can be identified by use of the percentage of trend. Cyclical components will show up as high or low percentage of trend values during years of expansion and contraction. Major irregular components will show up as one-time deviations.

Confidence in the accuracy of the trend is gained if the percentages of trend values are close to 100 percent, and the assumption can be made that the variation in actual collections is due to the underlying trend. In contrast, if the percentage of trend values varies significantly above or below 100 percent, many other factors might account for the collections, and your confidence in using the trend line to project will be weakened. A trend line must be approached with caution in such a case.

PROJECTION OF REVENUES FOR THE NEXT FISCAL YEAR

Each member of the budget staff will make a projection of revenues from each source for the City for the upcoming fiscal year (FY VI) based on data submitted during the revenue history presentation.

In reporting your revenue projections, use Forms 3 and 3A. Use Form 3 to array your revenue projections. After completing Forms 3 and 3A, make photocopies for your classmates and instructor and keep for use in Step 8, page 59.

For Form 3A, you should list each revenue source. Provide the following information for each revenue:

    a. Your rationale for choosing the projection method which you used. For instance, did you discern forthcoming changes in economic factors (retail sales, housing starts, personal income) or population increases which caused you to choose either a conservative or less conservative projection method?

    b. Your opinion on the effect of inflation, rate changes or new ways of billing that might have produced changes in the revenue line item in the past five years.

In listing projected revenues for Year VI, round off dollars to the nearest dollar. Calculate percentages to two decimal places to the right of the decimal point.

FORM 3

Your Name _____

Revenue Projections

Item of Revenue	Actual Revenue Year IV ($)	Actual Revenue Year V ($)	Projected Revenue Year VI ($)	Change between Year V and Year VI (Actual $)	Change between Year V and Year VI (%)

Your Name _____

Revenue Projection Justifications

For each revenue source, provide the following information: (a) your rationale for using the projection method chosen and (b) your opinion on the effect of inflation, etc., which might have produced the change in the revenue line item.

a.

b.

a.

b.

a.

b.

(Use more sheets as needed.)

Presentation and Analysis of Revenue Projections

OBJECTIVE

To determine collectively the revenues that the City reasonably may expect for the forthcoming fiscal year.

ACTION SEQUENCE

1. Written presentation of revenue projections
   a. Photocopy and distribute copies of your completed revenue projection report (Forms 3 and 3A from Step 7).
   b. Outline oral report on how revenue was projected, on page 59.

2. Analysis of projected revenues and consultation
   a. Review written reports (Forms 3 and 3A) from other staff members, dealing with their methods of revenue projections and their results. Consult with other staff members for minor clarifications.
   b. Analyze others' completed versions of Form 3 and develop questions dealing with similarities and differences in approaches and results.
   c. Record questions on page 60.

3. Oral presentation of revenue projections
   a. Present oral report on revenue projections and methods.
   b. Compare these reports and record your impressions on page 61. Focus on the advantages and disadvantages exhibited by different revenue projection methods.

4. Staff decision on revenue projections
   a. Reconcile revenue projections presented orally and distributed in earlier sessions.
   b. Record assumptions and methods employed in the reconciled projections on page 62.
   c. Prepare a written report on the revenue projection reconciliation.

PRESENTATION OF REVENUES FOR UPCOMING YEAR

In Step 7, you prepared a projection of revenues by line item on Forms 3 and 3A, outlining the City's expected revenues, source by source. The list of revenues should reflect the "history" of revenue collection prepared in Step 5. These forms should include a detailed explanation of the data on which the projections are based and the projection methods used. Photocopy the forms for other staff members, who will study and discuss the explanation later. Extensive comment is not required at this time. Be sure to pay attention to the earmarked revenues your department oversees.

As you prepare for your oral report to the budget staff, make a basic outline of the material and include it here.

ANALYSIS OF PROJECTIONS AND CONSULTATION

During the time between written and oral presentations, budget staff members analyze other staff members' projections (Forms 3 and 3A), preparing questions and/or counter-proposals. You will consult with one another, if necessary, to clarify information presented.

The analysis should focus on differences as well as similarities among projections. You should question assumptions made by other members, as well as their revenue projection methods.

After examining revenue projections made by other budget staff members, develop questions dealing with the major similarities and differences in their approaches and results and your own. Record those questions in the space provided here.

ORAL PRESENTATIONS OF REVENUE PROJECTIONS

After analyzing one another's reports, you will reconvene to explain your own revenue projections. Each of you, as staff members, will present his/her projections, field questions, and will defend assumptions and methods.

Different revenue projection methods exhibit particular advantages and disadvantages when used in conjunction with certain revenue sources. Did you notice any such characteristics? Record your observations here.

STAFF DECISION ON REVENUE PROJECTIONS

After completing oral presentations and discussion, all staff members will develop a composite revenue projection.

You first will work out differences among individual projections, basing the final projection on assumptions and methods on which staff members agree. Then prepare a written report detailing projected revenues (Form 3, revised) and explaining the assumptions and methods used in projecting revenues.

Explain here the assumptions and the methods (e.g., consensus, majority vote, etc.) employed by the budget staff in reconciling differences in revenue projections.

Estimating Capital Improvements

OBJECTIVE

To develop information for the capital improvements section of the City's annual operating budget and to design a one-year program incorporating large-scale projects—buildings, land, and equipment—for the next fiscal year.

ACTION SEQUENCE

1. In *Budgeting: Formulation and Execution,* read the following:
   a. Freeman, Niemi, and Wilson, "Evaluating Public Expenditures: A Guide for Local Officials"
   b. Miller, "Cost-Benefit Analysis"
   c. Vogt, "Budgeting Capital Outlays and Improvements"
   d. Chapman, "Capital Financing: A New Look at an Old Idea"
   e. Zino, "The Development of a Planned Debt Policy"
   f. Hildreth, "State and Local Governments as Borrowers: Strategic Choices and the Capital Market"
   g. Standard and Poor's, "Municipal Finance Criteria"
   h. Moody's Investors Service, "The Fundamentals of Revenue Bond Credit Analysis"
   i. California Debt Advisory Commission, "Competitive versus Negotiated Sale of Debt"
   j. California Debt Advisory Commission, "Understanding the Underwriting Spread"
   k. Mumford, "Techniques to Lower Municipal Borrowing Costs"
   l. California Debt Advisory Commission, "Types and Purposes of Lease Financing"
   m. Lee, "Life-Cycle Costing"
2. Read section on definitions and capital improvements/capital outlays on pages 64-65.

3. Review your departments' needs for capital improvements and capital outlays. Then, list the capital improvements for each assigned department on the "Inventory of Capital Projects" on page 66.

4. Read "Financing Capital Improvements" and "Setting Project Priorities" on pages 67-70.

5. Complete Form 4, page 71, for each capital improvement listed on "Inventory of Capital Projects."

6. Using pages 72-74, set capital improvements project priorities for each department by ranking each project listed on the "Inventory of Capital Projects" and described on Form 4.

IDENTIFYING CAPITAL IMPROVEMENTS

Definitions

A separate budget method, apart from the operating budget process, should be used to identify, schedule, and finance the capital improvements (capital outlays) of a municipality. The following definitions and explanations should be helpful.

Capital Improvements Projects: Capital improvements (capital outlays) are considered projects of generally large size, fixed nature, and long life, providing new or improved facilities or services. Some examples are street improvements, bridges, water mains and treatment facilities, sewers (storm and sanitary), public buildings, parks, playgrounds, libraries, recreational facilities, and the acquisition of land or rights-of-way related to these projects. Major replacements and reconstruction also should be considered capital improvements.

Certain types of new, major equipment also are considered capital improvements. As a rule of thumb, major equipment can be defined as heavy equipment with a life expectancy of at least 15 years. Examples of heavy equipment include fire apparatus (this equipment should be included for any new fire stations), bulldozers, and draglines.

Other capital improvements items are preconstruction architectural and engineering costs and consultative services (site-location studies, etc.) related to the planning and designing of projects.

Capital Improvements Program (or *Public Improvements Program*): The capital improvements program is a schedule of projects, ordered according to priorities for a 5- to 10-year period, along with estimated costs and sources of revenues. The most commonly used period for a capital improvements program is 6 years.

Capital Budget: The capital budget is included as the capital improvements section of the annual operating budget. It is composed of the government's capital outlays/capital improvements, which are major, nonrecurring expenditure(s), or any expenditures for physical facilities. For each, costs and usually sources of financing are given for the forthcoming fiscal year.

Advantages of Capital Improvements Budgeting

Capital improvements budgets not only represent the coming year's improvements, but also provide an orderly schedule of future improvements and a means for evaluating the long-range needs of the community. Capital budgeting goes beyond determining needs to providing a device for establishing priorities and analyzing the City's ability to pay for improvements. Capital budgeting has the following advantages of

1. preventing duplication of projects and equipment;
2. providing a vehicle for coordinating projects;
3. allowing sufficient time for the proper technical design of proposed projects;
4. establishing priorities, thereby assuring that the most essential improvements are provided first;
5. helping provide for an equitable distribution of public improvements throughout the community;
6. allowing maximum benefit from available public funds;
7. coordinating physical with financial planning;
8. providing a basis for formulating possible bond programs as well as a project pool for investigating various state and federal aid programs; and
9. providing citizens with information on long-range municipal projects and their potential costs, including the possible need for future bond programs.

How to Determine Capital Improvements Projects

In one way or another, a capital improvement always will affect the operating budget. Even though financing may come from a noncity source, there will be maintenance costs and other hidden costs (such as heating, air conditioning, and supplies). A government department should research these hidden costs in determining capital improvements projects to be undertaken.

To develop projects, departments should consider at least the following questions:

1. Is the proposed project one that will benefit the operation of the department?
2. Will the proposed project cost more to build, equip, and staff than the benefits (both tangible and intangible) that the citizens will realize from the project's worth?
3. Will professional standards prescribe certain projects?

Over the years, generally accepted standards have been developed for almost every function of local government. For example, the Insurance Services Office (ISO) has developed standards to help insurance companies determine if local governments have sufficient fire-protection facilities, equipment, and services. Similar approaches have been used to help local governments determine needs in service areas such as recreation, police, and water and sewer distribution. Publications of professional associations can help you identify the generally accepted guidelines.

INVENTORY OF CAPITAL PROJECTS

List the capital improvements projects for each department you study. You may increase or decrease the number and size of capital projects assigned to you in the *Data Sourcebook.*

Department	Capital Improvements	Justification

FINANCING CAPITAL IMPROVEMENTS

There are a number of ways to finance capital improvements projects. The most common methods used are described here.

Pay-As-You-Go

Pay-as-you-go means financing capital projects with current revenues—paying cash instead of borrowing against future revenues. The amount available for spending is the difference between what is collected currently and what is required for operating expenses and prudent reserves.

This method works well when capital needs are steady and modest, and financial capability is adequate. It can include appropriations in the budgets of two or more years, without borrowing, to pay for projects that take that time to build. Pay-as-you-go also can provide a fund for future expenditures by building sums in annual increments or by setting aside unanticipated, windfall income until the balance is large enough. Such a fund, it may be noted, will earn interest.

Pay-as-you-go has several advantages. First, it can save costs, depending on interest rates and repayment schedules. This is because interest on long-term bonds can more or less equal the original capital costs. Thus, one can pay twice for a capital improvement even though the annual bill over an extended period is disarmingly low.

Second, pay-as-you-go protects a government's borrowing capability for unforeseen major outlays that are beyond any current year's resources.

Third, pay-as-you-go avoids the inconvenience and considerable costs associated with marketing bond issues, such as those regarding advisors, legal counsel, and printing. However, pay-as-you-go when coupled with the regular, steady completion of capital improvements which are fully documented and publicized fosters favorable bond ratings when long-term financing is undertaken.

Fourth, pay-as-you-go puts a premium on advance planning. The multiyear capital improvements program allows not only for scheduling physical improvements prudently, but also for planning the financing to take advantage of accumulated surpluses, windfall income, and the realities of operating budget financing.

Despite its favorable characteristics, pay-as-you-go is by no means a panacea. It has both practical and theoretical disadvantages, some of which follow:

1. When projects are undertaken irregularly, rather than every year, pay-as-you-go puts a heavy burden on the project year budget. It creates awkward, fluctuating expenditure cycles that do not occur with extended financing.

2. A long-life asset should be paid for by its users throughout its normal life rather than all at once by those who may not be using it for the full term. The higher cost due to interest, spread over a larger number of users/payers, actually lowers the cost to all.

3. Since tax rates may have to be increased to pay for a series of capital improvements in a short period of time, pay-as-you-go would not be fair to people who move from the city after a brief residence. It would constitute a subsidy for those who come after the capital improvements program ends.

67

Municipal Bonds

The use of bond issues—borrowing—is the major alternative to "pay-as-you-go."

The decision to borrow turns on two basic choices: general obligation versus revenue bonds and long-term versus short-term borrowing.

In general, borrowing makes sense when the project (1) has a long, usable life such as a building, street construction, sewage disposal, or recreation facilities, or (2) can be financed by service charges to pay off revenue bonds.

Bond issues should be large enough to attract investors and small enough and short enough in duration to keep interest costs low. These lessons are learned either from experience or through the assistance of financial advisors, i.e., consulting firms in the business of helping municipalities plan and market long-term bond issues.

Financial advisors are of two kinds—those who assist but do not buy or sell and those who both assist and buy and sell bond issues. Fee structures, as well as the advisor's objectivity, i.e., whether the advisor will profit from the decision, will influence costs.

Although financial advisors will assist in determining market conditions and the most profitable strategy for selling bonds, the city usually faces state-imposed limits on indebtedness and special conditions on each type of bonding arrangement.

The first restriction concerns the amount of indebtedness. Many state constitutions limit indebtedness, General Obligation (G.O.) Bonds, to a specific percentage of the assessed value of all taxable property located within a municipality. This same provision also may stipulate that no new debt be incurred without the assent of a majority of qualified voters of the municipality. Not included in the city limitation is the indebtedness of the county, the school district, and most special-purpose districts and public authorities.

Most states stipulate that a municipality must provide for an annual tax sufficient to pay off the principal and interest within a specified number of years.

Special assessment bonds also may be restricted by the state. These bonds must be approved by the majority of the future project users. In some cities, state law requires that these bonds be retired within a specific number of years and that a city provide for default through attachment (foreclosure and seizure) of the users' property to satisfy the debt, since only the property owners who benefit from the improvement pay for the improvement.

State governments also restrict the use of revenue bonds. When these bonds are used for the purchase or construction of public works facilities that produce revenue, the municipality must repay the debt from revenue produced by the facility within a specified number of years.

Short-Term Notes

When local capital projects do not lend themselves to "pay-as-you-go" or bond financing, some municipalities have the legal authority to use short-term notes purchased by retail banking establishments or national securities' firms.

Advantages of short-term notes include the following:

1. A substantial lump sum can be borrowed at the moment of need and repaid in installments over the next few years.

2. A prospective bond issue can be shortened in years and reduced in amount with consequent interest savings.

68

3. There are not the extensive marketing costs associated with long-term bond issues, such as the expenses for bond counsel, printing, or paying agents.

State law may provide

1. that the aggregate amount of all these short-term borrowings not exceed a fixed percentage of the total property taxes collected in the preceding year;

2. that these loans be payable on or before the end of the calendar or fiscal year in which they are made;

3. that these loans may not be made in any year in which a prior loan is still unpaid; and

4. that the municipality cannot incur in any one calendar or fiscal year a total amount of loans in excess of anticipated revenue for that year.

Leases

Governments enter into contracts to use and possess equipment or property of another party for a specified time period. This financing method is termed a lease, and there are numerous advantages. Leasing is a way to acquire capital items, without the voter requirements and complexity associated with bond financing. Besides, some equipment has a short useful life which makes bond financing inappropriate. To lease equipment permits the government to use the item but not be responsible for its maintenance, depending upon the terms of the agreement.

Leases are used for duplication machines, vehicles, and even, in much more complicated arrangements, buildings and water/sewer system improvements. Leases are not defined as debt (with the associated stringent limits and approval requirements tied to debt obligations). This is achieved by including nonappropriation provisions in the agreements.

The typical nonappropriation clause states that, if the city does not appropriate funds for the lease payments in any given year the lease is terminated without being in default, but the city has to return the leased item. Of course, the leaseholder is unlikely to enter into a facility lease unless there is a high probability that the governmental unit will continue to make the yearly appropriations. This assurance is obtained after getting the government to agree not to substitute another asset for the one leased and by making sure the facility is essential to the ongoing performance of public services, and not one likely to be cast off easily.

Joint Financing

Many cities and counties find joint financing of a project useful. Examples include the construction of city-county office buildings, development of joint sanitary landfill sites, and funding of part of the costs of ambulance and fire-fighting equipment in exchange for services. This funding avenue should be explored.

State and Federal Aid

Historically, major funding sources for capital improvements have been federal assistance and state financial assistance. This type of funding arrangement should be explored extensively.

When considering federal or state aid, it is important that a city's established priorities be maintained. A project should not be undertaken just because funds are available. Since most aid programs require a match of local funds, a large number of nonpriority projects undertaken without adequate planning may impair seriously the financial condition of the municipality.

Privatization

Local governments are continuously challenged to ask fundamental questions on the appropriateness of providing a public service or whether the private marketplace should be left to gauge and resolve demand and supply. In those cases where governments determine that public provision is appropriate, the option of contracting for private production of that specific public service, subject to government specifications and oversight, still exists. As a result of such trends, privatization must be considered in any project financing, as well as in the financing of services in general. Joint public-private financing arrangements are possible, also.

Summary

Instead of financing capital improvements with bonds or a total "pay-as-you-go" plan, local officials often find combining the different financial schemes to be the best policy.

REQUEST FOR CAPITAL EXPENDITURES

(Construction, Repairs, or Modifications)

Use Form 4 to provide information concerning all proposed capital improvements projects *you believe* the department should undertake during the next fiscal year as listed on p. 66.

Detailed instructions for completing this form are as follows:

1. Title of Project: Specify the name of the proposed project requiring repair, modification, or construction.

2. Location: Specify the complete street address or other location of the project.

3. Description and Justification: Provide complete description of the proposed project and specify why it is needed. Include any results from analytical studies. Indicate the short- and long-term effects on the operating budget in particular.

4. Estimated Project Life.

5. Total Project Life Cost: Itemize all anticipated project expenditures including land, right-of-way (R.O.W.) fees, design costs, construction costs, repair or modification costs, and equipment, insurance, and interest costs. Also, indicate what funds will be required the first year.

6. Type of Funding Recommended: Decide what funding method you will recommend to finance the project.

FORM 4

Your Name _____

Request for Capital Expenditures
(Construction, Repair, or Modifications)

Department _____

NOTE: This form must be completed for each Capital Project and/or Building Repair

(1) Title of Project: _____

(2) Location: _____

(3) Description and Justification. Specify details concerning nature of the project and reasons it is required:

(4) Estimated Project Life: _____

(5) Total Project Life Cost:

Land, R.O.W. costs	$ _____
Design costs	_____
Construction costs	_____
Repair/Modification cost	_____
Equipment cost	_____
Insurance cost	_____
Interest	_____
Total	$ _____

First Year Cost: $ _____

(6) Type of Funding Recommended. Check one:

_____ Pay-as-you-go

_____ Municipal bond issue

_____ Lease

_____ Short-term note

_____ (Specify)

SETTING PROJECT PRIORITIES

After the determination and inventory of capital projects, the next step in preparing a capital budget is to arrange all the proposed projects into a sequence with the highest priority project at the top. You will list each department's projects on the next page.

To determine priorities, examine each proposed project in relation to the other projects. In this way, you can establish their relative priority.

The following criteria are sometimes used:

1. Highest priority projects are those required to
   a. complete or make fully usable an existing major capital facility;
   b. complete already programmed improvements;
   c. remedy a condition endangering the public health, safety, or welfare;
   d. provide facilities necessary for a critically needed community program; and
   e. achieve a minimal level of community services.

2. Lower priority projects are those used to
   a. conserve and improve facilities;
   b. achieve a standard level of community services;
   c. allow a growing, progressive area to stay in competition with other areas; and
   d. channel growth in a manner affordable to the government providing community services.

3. Lowest priority projects are those designed to
   a. raise community facilities and services to an optimum level;
   b. provide for the convenience and comfort of the public; and
   c. improve the social, cultural, economic, and aesthetic conditions of the community.

Of course, take into consideration the ability of the community to finance a particular project. In many towns and cities, this ability could result in a high priority being dropped out of the listing until financing becomes available.

After compiling information on each department's assigned projects, rank them by department with the highest priority project being ranked number one.

Department:

    1.

    2.

    3.

    4.

    5.

Department:

    1.

    2.

    3.

    4.

    5.

Department:

    1.

    2.

    3.

    4.

    5.

(Use more sheets as needed.)

In ranking each department's capital improvements, what ranking method did you employ? Describe your rationale for ranking one project higher than others.

Department:

Ranking Method and Rationale:

Department:

Ranking Method and Rationale:

Department:

Ranking Method and Rationale:

Department:

Ranking Method and Rationale:

(Use more sheets as needed.)

Developing Expenditure Estimates

OBJECTIVE

To estimate expenditures for each department that each staff member has already analyzed. The expenditure histories may now serve as a basis for estimating changes for the coming year. The capital budget information developed in Step 8 will be used as well, and personnel information will need to be prepared. Each staff member also may propose new projects, extensions, curtailments, or significant programmatic departures from present practices.

ACTION SEQUENCE

1. Review department expenditure history profiles prepared in Step 3, especially ones for your assigned department.

2. Review and analyze influences on the budget discussed in Step 2.

3. In *Budgeting: Formulation and Execution,* read the following selections *or* review those previously assigned.

   a. Proctor, "Six Steps for Communities in Crisis"

   b. Allan, "Evaluating Alternative Revenue Sources"

   c. Neels and Caggiano, "Pricing Public Services"

   d. Sanders and Tyer, "Local Government Financial and Budgetary Analysis"

   e. State of Rhode Island, "Monitoring Performance"

   f. Hyman and Allen, "Service Efforts and Accomplishments" (re: road maintenance)

   g. Friedman, "Calculating Compensation Costs"

   h. Coe, "Government Purchasing: The State of the Practice"

   i. Miller and Hildreth, "Advantages of a Risk Management Program"

   j. Hildreth and Miller, "Pension Policy, Management, and Analysis"

   k. Ammons, "Identifying Full Costs of a Program"

   l. Holzer and Halachmi, "Government as Competitor: Alternatives to Privatization"

4. Refer to the section called "City Personnel Data" in the *Data Sourcebook*. Review the "Classification Index" and "Scheduled Pay Allocations." Then, isolate the authorized positions and pay levels for each assigned department for the upcoming fiscal year.

5. Determine if any personnel actions (changes in classifications, new positions, deleting of existing positions) will be necessary to carry out the budget next year. If so, use Form 5 (*Workbook* p. 78) for recording such changes.

6. Formulate departmental budget requests, using Form 6 and Form 6A (pp. 80 and 81).

7. Justify the departmental budget requests in Form 7 (p. 83).

DETERMINING DEPARTMENTAL NEEDS

A critical function in budgeting is to develop realistic estimates of funding necessary to provide needed services for the upcoming fiscal year. The essential precondition is to have a firm understanding of the past spending practices of the department, current and future programmatic needs, and any other influences that may affect the costs of performing the service. Step 3 entailed the development of a five-year, past-spending profile for each department. Now, each staff member must prepare a statement of needed funding for the upcoming year for each department assigned under Step 3.

Consider the following factors in calculating expenditure estimates for each department analyzed in Step 3:

- general cost of items in present and prior years (for larger items the cost per unit should be used)
- price increases or adjustments, inflation
- changes in service
- requirements dictating the use of a particular item, including levels of new services
- legal requirements mandated by the federal or state governments, including cost-of-living salary increases
- promotions, deletions of positions, or other personnel position changes
- goals and objectives of departments

This type of analysis allows development of a budget request for each assigned department.

PERSONNEL REQUIREMENTS

A major part of a budget is personnel costs. Examinations of personnel requirements can be linked to the budget, especially in case of any changes from existing staff levels.

It is first necessary to determine the number, type, and salary requirements of all authorized positions in each assigned department(s) as of the end of fiscal year V. This information is contained in Section 3, "City Personnel Data," of the *Data Sourcebook*. Develop the baseline staffing profile (e.g., number of positions, salary totals) for the upcoming year (FY VI), using the information from the *Data Sourcebook*. Forecasting personnel expenditures calls for calculating all positions authorized at the start-of-the-year times their respective yearly pay. While this is the maximum amount to budget, actual expenditures reflect positions vacated during the year and replaced at different salary levels. This makes it difficult to use a staffing profile on a single day to replicate payroll expenses for past periods of time. Any proposed changes, such as additional or deleted positions, are to be made from the start-of-the-year position baseline.

Form 5 is used in making the following personnel changes:

1. To establish one or more new positions. The form also can be used to request more than one new person if all the proposed positions are for a new or expanded service program (for example, a new recreation center or branch fire station) and all the new positions are needed to institute the new program.

2. To change the classification and/or salary of existing position(s).

When submitting this form

a. read the instructions carefully before supplying the information required, and

b. complete each part of the form in full. This applies particularly to the justification section. Include appropriate measurements and other supporting data.

FORM 5

Your Name _____

Personnel Action Request

Department _____

PURPOSE OF FORM: This form is to be used to make the following personnel changes:

1. To establish new position(s).

2. To change job titles or salaries of existing position(s), including the deletion of existing positions.

1. Request to Establish New Position(s)

Number of identical positions requested _____ ; Duration: _____ Permanent _____

Temporary for _____ months

Title of Position(s)	Salary or Wage Level	Title of Position(s)	Salary or Wage Level

Justification for Position(s)

2. Request to Change (or Delete) Existing Position(s)

Number of identical positions _____ ; Action: change _____ delete _____

Present Title and Salary	Proposed Title and Salary (do not use if position is deleted)

Justification of Proposed Changes

Additional Cost Data Section

List the cost of additional equipment required if this request is approved.

Approval Section

_____ Date   _____ Date

_____ Approved _____ Disapproved   _____ Approved _____ Disapproved

_____   _____
Chief Executive   Governing Body

Submit this form for each position or group of identical positions.

BUDGET REQUESTS

Each departmental request for funding in the upcoming fiscal year must be presented on Form 6 and Form 6A or their equivalents.

On Form 6, present data according to the category of expenditures (e.g., salaries, supplies, services, capital outlays, capital improvements) used in Form 1. However, the specific line items requested depend on a number of factors, including (a) instructions which you are given regarding departmental requests in Part 2, "City Departments," of the *Data Sourcebook* and (b) the strategies which you decide to employ.

Form 6A can be used when footnotes or explanations are necessary to supplement data in Form 6. For example, if "supplies" are budgeted to increase by an amount likely to call unusual attention to the category, then it might be worthwhile to include some explanation or justification for the increase.

FORM 6

Summary of Expenditure Requests

Department _____

Categories and Line Items	Actual Year IV ($)	Actual Year V ($)	Requested Year VI ($)	Change between Year V and Year VI (Actual $)	Change between Year V and Year VI (%)

(Use more forms, if necessary; prepare Form 6A for "notes" required to accompany this form.)

FORM 6A

Your Name _____

Supplementary Notes

BENEFITS AND COSTS

Budget reviewers generally expect each department to prepare an overview sheet that presents the department's functions, objectives, and justifications for proposed capital expenditures.

To facilitate the presentation of this material, Form 7 should be prepared for each department. As much as possible, each major expenditure item should be justified in terms of a ratio of costs to benefits.

Thus, the key is to develop explicit goals and objectives for each department and then to relate the proposed expenditures to the announced goals/objectives.

FORM 7

Your Name _____

Summary of Benefits and Costs
Department _____

1. Description of departmental functions and responsibilities

2. Objectives for the forthcoming budget year

3. Summary of benefits

4. Summary of costs

Presentation and Analysis of Expenditure Proposals

OBJECTIVE

To prepare individual reports on proposed expenditures for each of your departments and to present these reports orally.

ACTION SEQUENCE

1. Presentation of written expenditure proposals without comments
   a. Distribute photocopies of all expenditure and personnel forms.
   b. Outline oral report on how expenditures were estimated for each department on *Workbook* page 86.

2. Analysis of proposed budgets and consultation and comparisons of calculations
   a. Review and analyze written reports from other staff members dealing with their proposed expenditures. In evaluating these expenditures, you may use the "Budget Review Checklist" on pages 90-91.
   b. Consult with other staff members for minor clarifications of information in the report when needed.
   c. Develop questions dealing with similarities and differences concerning approaches and results in the reports.
   d. Record questions on page 87.

3. Oral presentation of proposed budgets
   a. Present your oral report on departmental expenditure requests.
   b. Compare oral reports and record comments made regarding your proposals on page 88.

4. Research and consultation
   a. Review your expenditure proposals in terms of questions raised by other staff members.

b. Revise expenditure proposals as appropriate.

c. Record changes made to proposals, including revised assumptions, answers to other staff members' questions, and data recomputations on page 89.

PRESENTATION OF BUDGET FOR UPCOMING YEAR

Prepare a written report describing the expenditure requests for the department(s) studied and including detailed justifications for both operating and capital expenditures. This report will be studied and discussed later by other staff members; therefore, comment at this time is not required.

Attach a copy of the written report to this volume.

Below, include a basic outline of the material you plan to give orally to the budget staff.

COMPARISON OF CALCULATIONS

Compare other departments' expenditure proposals with your own. Reflect upon the different assumptions employed in calculations and basic data approaches. Record questions to be raised with individual staff members and/or the entire budget staff.

ORAL PRESENTATION OF PROPOSED BUDGETS

Each staff member will now present his/her budget proposals and concentrate on the justifications of the proposed expenditures. After this presentation, you should field questions about the proposals from other members. Budget staff personnel should be prepared to submit further justification of expenditure requests and/or further research at the conclusion of this presentation.

At the conclusion, break for further research and/or consultation.

Record any comments by other staff members about your expenditure proposals.

RESEARCH AND CONSULTATION

After submitting budget proposals to the staff, you will have the opportunity to propose written answers to questions raised earlier during the oral presentation or to formulate additional justifications of expenditure proposals. You also might revise your own proposals, in light of group decisions, decreasing or increasing amounts as appropriate.

Record any changes in your expenditure proposals brought about by feedback from others in the space below.

BUDGET REVIEW CHECKLIST

by Arthur B. Mohor, Jr.

Following is a list of questions to be considered when reviewing departmental requests. Well-prepared departmental estimates based on these points will facilitate the coordination of various budget estimates into a sound comprehensive operating plan for all municipal services. Consideration of these points will simplify the decisions to balance this plan of action with the municipality's ability to pay.

Programs

1. Have work programs been defined?
2. Have the objectives of new and expanded programs been defined clearly?
3. Have all increases or decreases been explained?
4. Has attention been given to long-run economy?
5. Have new sources of revenue been suggested to support new and expanded programs?
6. Have efforts been made to reduce costs through improved work methods, mechanization, or better personnel utilization?
7. Have priorities been assigned to new and expanded programs and to equipment?
8. Have the fees for rendering services been compared to the cost of rendering the service enforcing the regulations?
9. Have major problems encountered during the year been explained?
10. Have economies achieved during the past year by improving work methods been explained?
11. Are there any recommendations for further reducing costs and increasing the efficiency of the operation?
12. Are there any recommendations regarding changes in the level of services?
13. What were the effects of budgetary limitations last year?

Personnel

14. To what extent do the requested positions relate to defined activities and programs? Does an understanding or evaluation of duties and responsibilities warrant the need for new positions?
15. Have provisions been made for delay in filling new and vacant positions?
16. Does the opening of new capital facilities justify the need for the personnel in the operating budget?
17. Have employee turnover, overtime, seasonal personnel, leaves of absence, and the need for related appropriations been considered?

Service

18. Regarding contractual services, have expenditures and workload data of previous years been examined carefully?

19. For each specific service to be rendered, is the need and the manner of pricing explained? Has the level of service been examined to evaluate present methods?

20. Are contributions to nongovernmental agencies based on requests supported by detailed information about the service being provided? Has the effectiveness of such services been evaluated?

Materials and Supplies

21. Is an analysis of the expenditures and consumption of previous years included with requests for materials and supplies?

22. Have price increases and supplies required by additional personnel been considered? Does the need for additional supplies relate to increased workload or new and expanded programs? Have inventories been reviewed?

23. Are there inventory or other controls over the use of supplies? Have work methods been evaluated along with the type and quality of supplies?

Equipment

24. Has equipment been identified as replacement or new? Has the condition of the equipment being replaced, as well as its potential trade-in value, been reviewed? Have inventories of existing equipment been checked to determine the need for new equipment?

25. Have work methods, as well as the experience of other municipalities in using special types of equipment, been reviewed? Are requests for new equipment compatible with expanded work programs or to possible savings?

26. Have equipment needs of new personnel been considered?

27. Have repair costs, along with the advantages of leasing, been analyzed?

Preparation of Budget Draft

OBJECTIVE

To reconcile individual department requests with projected revenues, and to prepare a budget draft.

ACTION SEQUENCE

1. Read Levine, "Cutback Management in an Era of Scarcity."
2. Meet with staff members to reconcile the total amount of expenditure requests (Form 6) with the previously decided revenue projections (Form 3, revised). Note changes necessary to achieve a balanced budget on *Workbook* page 93.
3. Using Form 8 on page 96, "Expenditure Requests: Year VI," and after making the changes in line-item requests as may be required on Form 6 because of reconciliation, list expenditure requests by department for Year VI.
4. Make any required changes in Form 4, "Request for Capital Expenditures," Form 5, "Personnel Action Request," and Form 7, "Summary of Benefits and Costs," as may be necessary after reconciliation.
5. Make sufficient photocopies of Form 8, with attachments (revised Forms 4, 5, and 7), for everyone.
6. As a staff, compose a letter of transmittal.
7. Submit to the assistant to the mayor the budget package composed of (a) the letter of transmittal, (b) departmental expenditure requests for Year VI (Form 8 with attachments), and (c) projected revenues for Year VI (Form 3, revised).

BUDGET RECONCILIATION

The budget staff must prepare a balanced budget for Year VI. To accomplish this goal, the staff must compare the total Year VI expenditure requests for all departments (Form 6) with the projected revenues for Year VI (Form 3, revised).

ACHIEVING A BALANCED BUDGET

Municipalities must balance their proposed expenditures with forecasted revenues. The balanced budget rule typically imposes a legal constraint that forces decisions on both revenues and expenditures.

Record here what changes were required to achieve a balanced budget. What did it take for the budget staff to arrive at this result?

REVISING EXPENDITURE REQUESTS

Once a reconciliation has been made between expenditure requests and projected revenues, changes may be required in departmental budget requests. Form 8, "Expenditure Requests: Year VI," should be completed for each department whether there has been a change in the requests or not. A sample Form 8 is provided.

Copies of Form 8, with revised (as necessary) attachments—Form 4, "Request for Capital Expenditures," Form 5, "Personnel Action Request," and Form 7, "Summary of Benefits and Costs"—should be prepared for each class member.

Your Name _____

Expenditure Requests: Year VI
Department: Sanitation-Garbage Collection

Categories and Line Items	Actual Expenditure Year V ($)	Requested Expenditure Year VI ($)	Change between Year V and Year VI (Actual $)	Change between Year V and Year VI (%)
Salaries				
Salaries	424,624	464,569	39,945	9.41
Benefits	—	162,599	162,599	100
Subtotal	424,624	627,169	202,544	47.7
Supplies				
Gas and oil	54,186	35,000	22,186	(−38.8)
Tires, tubes & batteries	—	10,000	10,000	100
Tools & supplies	—	10,000	10,000	100
Janitorial supplies	—	2,500	2,500	100
Office supplies	20,268	5,000	(15,268)	(75.3)
Safety clothing	—	7,312	7,312	100
Subtotal	77,455	68,812	(7,642)	(10)
Services				
Communications	378	400	21	5.8
Freight and express	67	100	32	47.9
Travel	161	150	(11)	(−7.1)
Equipment repair	—	50,000	50,000	100
Local container repair	—	10,000	10,000	100
Real property repair	—	2,500	2,500	100
Utilities	4,265	4,500	234	5.5
Dues and subscriptions	35	40	5	14.3
Training	63	200	137	17.5
Professional services	739	750	10	1.4
Claims	—	1,500	1,500	100
Subtotal	5,710	7,014		
Capital Improvements				
(1) Rear-end loader	—	42,000	42,000	100
(1) Scooter	—	4,000	4,000	100
Subtotal	90,147	46,000	(44,147)	−49
Grand Total of Expenditures	597,937	813,121	215,184	36

Your Name _____

Expenditure Requests: Year VI

Department: _____

Categories	Actual Expenditure Year V ($)	Requested Expenditure Year VI ($)	Change between Year V and Year VI (Actual $)	Change between Year V and Year VI (%)

PRESENTATION OF BUDGET NARRATIVE: LETTER OF TRANSMITTAL

This phase marks the presentation of the official budget to the assistant to the mayor. Be ready to supply adequate supporting details.

Preparing a budget staff letter of transmittal is an important part of presenting the budget. This letter, which is an explanatory statement, should be a part of the official budget draft. This statement summarizes the proposed budget and the preceding year's budget and expenditures. It should also

1. explain increases and decreases in services;

2. explain and justify new and expanded programs;

3. compare the proposed budget with the FY V current budget and explain differences;

4. review the status of current programs and projects, including problems and accomplishments;

5. explain the extent to which capital projects will be financed on a pay-as-you-go basis (discuss any proposed increases in debt and their effects on the budget);

6. review and explain major increases and decreases in revenue as well as any proposed new sources;

7. discuss the impact of the budget on the tax base and the overall financial condition of the community;

8. summarize programs and projections that are important but that were not included in the budget;

9. state the expected end-of-year fund balance for each fund used by this City; and

10. confirm that revenues meet or exceed budgeted expenditures—that it is a balanced budget. It should also meet all legal requirements, including, but not limited to, the appropriate use of earmarked funds.

After a letter of transmittal has been written, the budget package should be submitted to the assistant to the mayor. It should include

1. the letter of transmittal,

2. budget requests for Year VI (Form 8, with attachments), and

3. projected revenue for Year VI (Form 3, revised).

Comments by Assistant to the Mayor and Staff Response

OBJECTIVE

To prepare a final version of the budget document for submission to the mayor. Revisions to draft may be made after comments of the assistant to the mayor.

ACTION SEQUENCE

1. Receive comments on the budget draft from the assistant to the mayor, who has received the staff's budget. Ask any necessary questions.

2. In light of the assistant to the mayor's comments, collectively revise the parts of the package—the letter of transmittal, the expenditure proposals, and the revenue projections—when appropriate or necessary.

3. Record on pages 99-100 the comments made by the assistant to the mayor concerning the staff's budget and note what changes in the budget were made by the staff due to these comments.

4. Resubmit the revised package—the budget draft including the letter of transmittal, the expenditure proposals by department, and the revenue projections—to the assistant to the mayor by the budget deadline.

What comments were given by the assistant to the mayor after reviewing the budget document?

What changes in the budget were brought about by comments by the assistant to the mayor?

Feedback Session— Assessing Budget Formulation and Execution

OBJECTIVE

To review and comment upon the budgeting laboratory, evaluating what has been learned through the information on budgeting as well as the process of designing a city budget; to explore key items in budget execution.

ACTION SEQUENCE

1. Discuss with other staff members the events that happened while they developed the budget package (how differences were resolved, etc.)

2. Assess the helpfulness of the budgeting information contained in *Budgeting: Formulation and Execution* in conducting the various laboratory steps.

3. Record changes in the budget-making process that you would want incorporated if you had to prepare a budget for a succeeding budget year.

4. In *Budgeting: Formulation and Execution,* read the following selections *or* review those previously assigned.

   a. Forrester and Mullins, "Rebudgeting: The Serial Nature of Municipal Budgetary Processes"

   b. Proctor, "Six Steps for Communities in Crisis"

   c. Khan, "Cash Management: Basic Principles and Guidelines"

   d. Miller and Hildreth, "Advantages of a Risk Management Program"

   e. Allan, "Unreserved Fund Balance and Local Government Finance"

   f. Price Waterhouse and Company, "Understanding Local Government Financial Statements"

   g. Brown, "The 10-Point Test of Financial Condition: Toward an Easy-to-Use Assessment Tool for Small Cities"

   h. Zehms, "Proposed Financial Ratios for Use in Analysis of Municipal Annual Financial Reports"

   i. Sorensen, Hanbery, and Kucik, "Managerial Accounting"

j. U.S. General Accounting Office, "Government Auditing Standards"

k. State of Massachusetts, "The Municipal Audit: Choice and Opportunity"

l. Brooks and Pariser, "Local Government Accountability and the Need for Audit Follow-Up"

5. Answer the questions on the following pages regarding budget execution.

Why and how are budgets revised during the year?

Discuss how you would track cash and cash needs over the fiscal year as you execute the budget.

What will it take to implement a managerial accounting system so that the cost of each city service can be utilized in the budgetary process?

How are physical assets protected from loss, and what are the budgetary implications of risk management programs?

What are the differences between budgets and end-of-year financial statements?

What information could be gained from audited end-of-year financial statements for use in subsequent budgets?

What is the importance of a fund balance, and how can it grow beyond what was expected?

What financial ratios, in general, and for this municipality specifically, signal fiscal stress?

What problems (if any) would you anticipate the auditors noting about FY V *and* FY VI results?

How does an audit produce accountability?

Why does a government need an audit follow-up?

Assess the city's credit quality for FY VI.

Evaluate the usefulness of the budgeting laboratory.

NOTES _____

NOTES _____

NOTES _____

NOTES _____

NOTES

NOTES

NOTES _____

NOTES

NOTES